Complete 180:
A Journal for Cultivating Self-Love After a Breakup

Jessica A. Hutton

Complete 180

Copyright 2018 © by Jessica A. Hutton

All rights reserved.

No part of this publication may be reproduced, distributed or transmitted in any form or by any means, including photocopying, recording, or any other electronic or mechanical methods, without the prior written permission of the publisher, except in the case of brief quotations embodied in critical reviews and certain other noncommercial uses permitted by copyright law.

Links to other resources have been provided in this book. Neither the author nor the publisher can be held responsible for any content contained on those links. Any link to an outside resource does not indicate endorsement of that resource, and does not necessarily reflect the policies, opinions, or practices of the author or the publisher.

Although I am a licensed social worker, I am not your social worker. The advice and strategies found within may not be suitable for every situation and is strictly for educational and informational purposes only. Nothing you read in this book is meant to diagnose, substitute for, or otherwise replace actual face-to-face professional counseling. This work is sold with the understanding that neither the author nor the publisher are held responsible for any action taken by any person as a result of viewing or otherwise obtaining information from this book or the results accrued from the advice in this book. Thus, if you wish to apply ideas contained in this book, you are taking full responsibility for your actions.

Images from Shutterstock.

ISBN-13: 978-1982060138

ISBN-10: 1982060131

Printed in the United States of America.

DEDICATION

To the one whose unwavering belief in me helped to keep me feeling inspired in my darkest hours.
And for all of you, who want to be healed from your past, liberated to experience a brighter future, and made whole from within as you fall deeper in love with yourself…this is for you.

CONTENTS

Dedication	i
Preface	
How I Love Myself	14
I AM Collage	27
Develop Your Personal Vision and Mission Statements	38
Mirror, Mirror	50
My Feelings Chart	62
How I Loved You	70
Baggage Claim	77
A Letter to My Ex	89
My Breakup Safety Plan	100
My Self-Care Action Plan	111
How I Feel Safe in Romantic Partnerships	123
How You Loved Me	125

Spring Clean Your Life	137
Love Letter to Self	148
Home Spa Day	159
Compliment Jar	170
How I Need to Be Loved	175
Reframing	183
21 Days of Self-Care	194
Now What?	227

PREFACE

I knew I had lost myself as I laid on a filthy extended stay hotel floor, curled into the fetal position, and weeping incessantly because I had lost someone with whom I had absolutely no interest in creating a life with. He was my rebound guy, but it felt more like a boomerang experience as I had been hit by his wanton disregard of my thoughts, feelings, time, and body, and had somehow convinced myself that I could do no better than him.

It had only been one month since I left a four-year relationship with someone I had loved dearly and was engaged to. I told myself and my partner that our relationship must end because I was overcome by a feeling that something was missing in my life and believed that I could only discover what it was if I started seeing other people. My fiancé owned the home we lived in together, and since I had begun openly seeing someone else while residing there, they decided it would be best if I moved out immediately, so I did. I was a single mother, jobless, and had nothing but my credit cards to keep me afloat. I needed a job, a home for my son and me, and a miracle, but instead I cleaved to my rebound guy and the idea that my life would somehow become better with him in it.

Every day I clung to my rebound and in return I was left waiting for his calls and text messages that he persistently promised but never delivered. Sometimes I sat for hours at a time, like I had when I was an adolescent, waiting for him to either pick me up or meet me for a date that he asked me out on but either showed up late for or not at all. I frequently begged in vain for him to talk with me about something substantive and relevant, and all this time I wondered why I was putting up with this "relationship" when it was quite evident that we had mutual disinterest in each other and were a poor fit. Nevertheless, I wept. I was close to maxing out three credit cards as I was charged weekly for my stay at the hotel and had relied on Chipotle for lunch and dinner because there was no stove in my room and I had wanted some sort of comfort. Finally, to add insult to injury, my son was two-thousand miles away spending time with his father because I was unable to provide a home for him, was uncomfortable with him having to stay in the hotel all summer and needed the time to find a way to secure a home for us. So, after several nights of interminable weeping on the dirty hotel floor feeling sorry for myself, I got up and decided to take a long, hot shower. In that shower, as the steam boxed out the bathroom, my naptural curls shrank from the moisture and heat, and I felt the sweltry mix of sweat and piping hot water dripping from my head and cascading down my curves, I had a revelation...

My relationships reflect me and all my mess.

I had begun dating and having sex when I was fourteen years old and had spent nearly two decades, with dozens of sexual partners, trying to create a love that I was not equipped to give or receive. After all that, I finally realized how extremely disappointed and desperately unfulfilled I had been chasing love outside myself. I couldn't recall any time I had experienced joy in my relationships and was only able to muster up very few memories of happiness; suddenly, it dawned on me that all this time I had blamed my partners for not being or providing enough to enrich my spirit, soul and body, when the truth is that I could neither discern or receive from them any gift of real love or satisfaction because I was not in love or satisfied with myself. I realized that I had unconsciously blamed every partner I shared my time with for not making me whole. And then I cried once more because I learned that I thoroughly unhappy with who I was inside and out, and because I apparently had the responsibility to cultivate self-love but didn't believe I was spiritually, psychologically or emotionally equipped to do so.

So, as much as I longed for unconditional love, affection, commitment, passion, great sex and all the other benefits that can come with healthy romantic partnerships, I understood that I could never attain and sustain any of that until I returned to my first love – myself. I decided that I needed to get my sh** together and come home to myself in spirit, soul and body and that required me to take the time to figure out how to love me. I needed to examine the breadth and depth to which I perceived my value and worth; to explore the frequency at which I treated myself with compassion, grace, forgiveness and mercy; and to practice feeling content and grateful with being alone. Accordingly, being the analytical problem-solver that I am, I decided to develop a series of questions to help me evaluate my past relationships and my role in their development, destruction and ultimate demise. I was intent on discovering patterns that revealed my thoughts, feelings and beliefs about relationships and how all the relationships I experienced impacted the way I engaged with different partners at different times in my life. The data I collected by answering the initial set of questions I wrote was helpful, albeit incomplete, as none of it revealed anything about how I felt about myself apart from any romantic relationship. That prompted the development of the self-love questions and later questions concerning personal accountability, core values and beliefs, and others that really exposed my vulnerabilities.

French philosopher and priest, Pierre Teilhard de Chardin said that "We are not human beings having a spiritual experience. We are spiritual beings having a human experience." You will find that I have referenced the spirit, soul and body throughout *Complete 180*.

To be a spiritual being having a human experience means that our bodies are mere cases of flesh that house the essence of our true selves - the spirit and the soul. It is with our bodies that we have a palpable experience of our world, as we engage it with our five senses which are smell, touch, taste, sight, and hearing. The body is the part of us that tends to feel most real and relevant, and yet, it is inexorably subject to the dictates of our spirit and soul, regardless of their state. Therefore, when we first meet someone we are attracted to, we experience various sensations in our bodies such as blushing, rapid heartbeat, dry mouth, or sweating, which confirm our attraction to the individual based on the dictates of our soul. Inside, different components of the soul have concluded that the individual has potential to meet some of our needs and, so we decide to go on a date with them to explore them deeper. On the flip side, when we experience a breakup, we may experience physical sensations such as loss of appetite, insomnia, nausea, rapid heartbeat or bruxism, because our souls are in a state of distress and yield a psychosomatic response.

The soul is the part of human beings where we carry our intangible albeit unique essence. Many of our lives are navigated by our souls because our soul is comprised of our emotions, thoughts, and interpretations of the world. Our soul contains our consciousness and it guides our decision-making processes. With our souls we are able to recognize our unique identities, core values, and beliefs and live according to our own will. We go to therapists, journal, read self-help books, and fall in love because of our souls and since your soul has been attacked by heartache, you have picked up this book in the hopes that it can help facilitate the healing of your soul so that you may return to your most vibrant self and finally move on with your life.

Last, but certainly not least, is the spirit. The spirit part of human beings is the part that connects us to God. To be a spiritual being having a human experience is to be made in the image of God, and to be made in the image of God, is to possess His character, His ability, and His mind devoid of a physical structure that is the body. From a Christian standpoint, it is the image of God that all human beings carry which truly identifies who we are and justifies our usage of "I Am." Thus, anything we believe, think or speak following the words "I Am" becomes our truth - for better or worse - because "I Am" is a spiritual decree which manifests tangible things, and this is so because "I Am" for God represents His abiding inability to deny Himself, which is why His words become flesh. Even though a lot of us are not in touch with our spiritual selves, it remains the most poignant aspect of our existence. When people reference the subconscious and intuition, they are revealing the functions of our spirit which possesses a knowing inexplicable to the soul, and yet, is somehow confirmed through the activation of our body's senses and other manifest things. Our spiritual being is the part of us that yearns for love and connection and was created with the natural ability to release it and receive it according to God's image. Unfortunately, because we experience so much trauma in our lives, our souls develop a resistance to the natural process of releasing and receiving love, and consequently, we find ourselves in unfulfilling relationships that result in painful breakups.

Although this book will not expound on the characteristics of each part of the human experience, they are nonetheless referenced to help you gauge your self-awareness about each aspect of your being that sets you apart from all others. Hold on to the descriptions of each part of your identity that I've identified above so that you can answer the applicable questions reflectively and with full understanding.

It's been said that it takes 21 days to develop a habit and 90 days to create a lifestyle; *Complete 180* is a personal workbook and journal that will help you change your habits and improve your lifestyle if you use it intentionally for the next 180 days. I encourage you to spend all 180 days engaging in deep reflection, outside of your journaling time, so that you can learn who you truly are, fall in love with yourself and enjoy being single. This personal workbook and journal is broken up into four vantage points that contain questions you will answer about yourself as you relate to the vantage point being presented. These four vantage points are *How I Love Myself, How I Loved You, How You Loved Me,* and *How I Need to be Loved.* Each section contains forty-five days of journal prompts with the idea that when you have completed the journal, you will have experienced a 180 transformation in your soul, learned to honor and respect your body, and been awakened to your spiritual self. When I allowed myself to sit in my thoughts and feelings without expectation or judgment, I found my truest self and felt liberated with every stroke of my pen. I implore you to do the same by engaging in honest self-reflection throughout the process and by responding to each prompt truthfully, as it will open your eyes to the underline issues that create problems in and ultimately result in the demise of your romantic relationships.

From the vantage point of *"How I Love Myself"* you will evaluate your perception of self and the way you understand and affirm your value and worth, exercise self-compassion and grace, and demonstrate respect and honor for self in your thoughts, beliefs, speech and behaviors. In this section you will answer a few questions about how your self-regard was impacted after your relationship, but the primary focus is on the self. In this section you will have the opportunity to be reminded about how much you love yourself, what it is about you that makes you great without a lover, and what action steps you can take to continue your personal development.

From the vantage point of *"How I Loved You,"* you will evaluate your role in the development, deconstruction and demise of your relationship. The promptings in this section will enable you to think critically about your relationship behavior patterns and how they may affect your intrapersonal relationships, and then identify alternative thought patterns and behaviors that may help you cultivate stronger, more secure and stable relationships.

The next vantage point, *"How You Loved Me,"* focuses on the self as you perceive the ex. This section is interesting because it permits solution-based venting. You get to express all the issues you had with your ex and then you are given the opportunity to take a step back and figure out how the way you perceive yourself may have influenced the way they treated you. If you completed the prior two vantage points honestly and thoroughly you should be better equipped to respond to the prompts in this section. Some may be more challenging than others and may elicit unexpected emotional responses, I encourage you to embrace your vulnerability and dive into the process. Don't feel confined to the questions provided. Feel free to expound on your thoughts and feelings as needed and ask yourself additional questions that lead to deeper reflection and emotional catharsis. Once you can acknowledge and learn to accept and even appreciate your past relationships and exes, it becomes much easier to let go of what was and move on with your life. Even better still, it's much easier to focus on self-love.

Finally, the last section of the book, *"How I Need to Be Loved,"* is from the vantage point of the self in a prospective long-term partnership. In this section you will refer to all the significant relationships of your past to evaluate how well you interact with people in intimate relationships and then determine what must be changed about you so that you can have a healthy partnership that lasts a lifetime. You will explore your relationship values and preferences, become attuned to your relationship behaviors and communication styles, and identify what you really need in a lifelong partner. This section is fun and it's also challenging and eye-opening. Even though you may have some idea what you want in a lifelong partnership, don't jump ahead of yourself. Take the forty-five days afforded you in this section to meditate and get in tune with your spirituality so that you may gain access to that inexplicable knowledge necessary to practice discerning, mature and natural love. Complete this vantage point in recognition of its self-honoring qualities and know that self-love involves engaging in behaviors that encourage the development of self-awareness.

Complete 180 also contains fifteen activity prompts with a different self-love focus. The activities are scheduled ten days apart, however, because they are not necessarily attached to any vantage point, you can complete them as needed without interfering with the guided journaling healing process. The fifteen self-love focuses include: positive self-talk; intentional living; body love; self-awareness; accountability and responsibility; catharsis; self-regulation; self-care; healthy boundaries; new beginnings; positive self-regard; personal intimacy; self-confidence; positive reframing; and self-care habituation.

Take each vantage point seriously. You will find that when you take the time to consult your own spirit and soul in a quiet space, that you will find all the answers you need to achieve holistic healing and self-love. You will realize how all things and people are connected and that even though it may hurt like hell in the meantime, all things truly may work out for your good. Just trust the process, release your faith and know that things will get better for you and you will get past your ex and your breakup.

Thank you for choosing *Complete 180: A Journal for Cultivating Self-Love After a Breakup*. You are on the right track to reclaiming your life and your heart. I support you on this journey as you journal your way to freedom from your past relationship and return to your first real love that is you.

With all my love,
Jessica A. Hutton

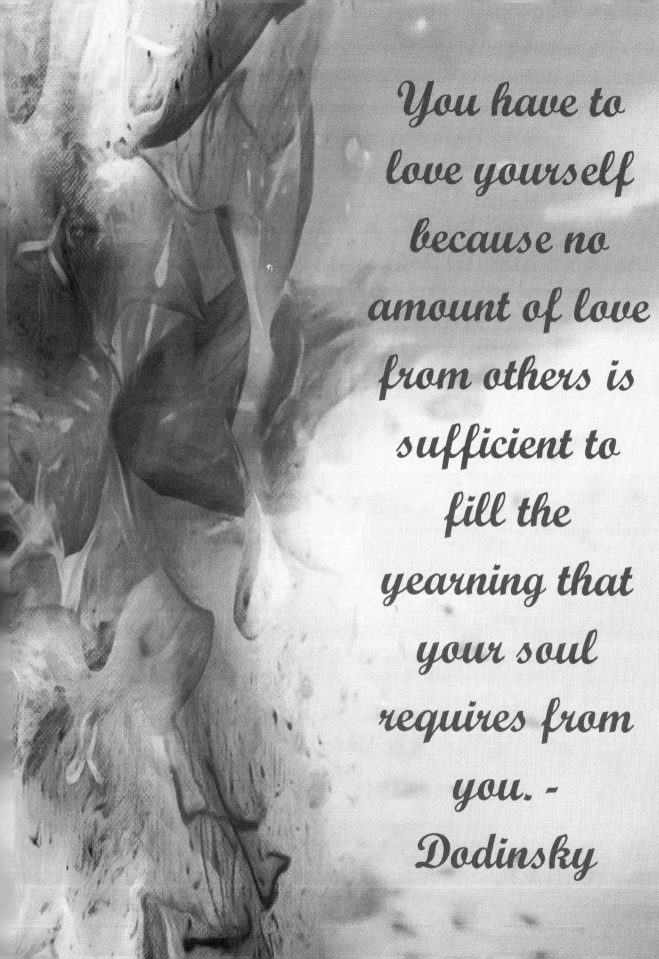

You have to love yourself because no amount of love from others is sufficient to fill the yearning that your soul requires from you. - Dodinsky

HOW I LOVE MYSELF

Break ups suck. Heartache is worse. And yet, having been through several dozen breakups in my three decades of wild living, I know two things to be true: 1) You will get past this breakup, whether you've experienced this kind of pain before or not; and 2) Getting past your breakup is more meaningful if you use the time alone to return to your first true love…you.

Initially when my fiancée and I broke up I thought that I wasn't fazed by it. I was ready to move on from what I thought was an unfulfilling relationship, and since we had been rejected by our inner circles for being a lesbian couple, I also thought I was making a decision that would finally draw love and acceptance into my life. Unfortunately, I got involved with a man who blatantly disrespected me and seemed to have no intention or even the ability to love me, so when I found myself crying after this man who was completely wrong for me when it made more sense to be crying over the loss of a woman I had loved dearly for four years of my life and had been engaged to marry, I knew that I had completely lost myself and that the only way I could find me was to do something I had never done before - be single. So, I was single… and then my ex-fiancée found someone new.

I had battled depression, suicidal ideations and other very dark emotions and experiences for years but learning that my ex-fiancée was involved with someone else sunk me to a lower place that I didn't recognize and felt that I was incapable of climbing out of. Most nights I couldn't breathe and could only manage to sleep about two hours. I could only handle eating one meal a day before I felt sick and had shed approximately twenty pounds from my one-hundred and ninety-pound frame, which should have flattered me, but instead made me look like Jack Skellington because of the darkness I carried in my broken soul. I obsessively called and texted my ex-fiancée, begging her to answer, and when her girlfriend was tired of me interrupting their time together, I'd find myself in shouting matches with her and calling her horrific names. This time I hadn't lost myself, I was gone. My health waned in my three-part being and I thought that I wanted to die. I wasn't nourishing my body, which exacerbated the weakness I was already enduring as a symptom of my dejected soul. I had convinced myself that I was impervious to any positive effect that my safety and self-care plans were intended to produce. And I refused to employ any religious or spiritual practice partly because I feared it would work and I preferred to be depressed, and partly because I was angry with God for allowing me to lose someone I now realized I didn't want to live without - and to someone else, for that matter.

Needless to say, I didn't think it was possible to return to myself and achieve peace within my soul until I miraculously woke up the morning after Christmas with a new mind. I took a long, hot shower in my own cozy bathroom, like I had done at the extended-stay hotel nearly eight months prior, and then prayed for God to help me accept my ex-fiancée's new life and give me the grace to begin my own. I then called my ex fiancée to apologize for all the pain I caused her and her new partner - she apologized just the same and we both received closure. Shortly thereafter, she ended the relationship with her new partner and we recommitted to each other. Our relationship lasted eight months and I broke up with her again because of the same gnawing feeling that I was missing something, only this time, neither of us ran into the arms of anyone else. We both committed to being single and to actively practicing our faith, spirituality and self-love so that our psychological, emotional and spiritual health might become steadfast.

The hardest thing about enduring a breakup is trying to find a way to manage the pain. It seems like heartbreak leaves an indelible impression on our souls that prohibits us from letting go of what was or might have been and seeking the possibilities before us. It's as though we become incapacitated and surrender to the dismal fate of eternal loneliness, anhedonia, and despair. Before I was involved with my ex-fiancée, I didn't know how to be single and it became more evident after we had broken up and I lost my mind. I had been dating and/or sexually involved with someone since I was fourteen years old and I had a child when I was fifteen. I didn't have to be alone and I most certainly didn't want to be. Nevertheless, as I got older my dating pool seemed to get smaller and I found myself either staying in dead-end, long-term relationships or obsessing over fantasy-driven short-term relationships and unrequited crushes. I didn't even know how to be single in my mind. Then, as I began to meditate on the kinds of writing prompts I needed to develop so I could process my thoughts and emotions about my past relationships, I conducted an Internet search for the definition of single so that I could get a firm grasp on where to start this journey. Unfortunately, none of the definitions I found resonated with me, however, I did come across synonyms for the word that are very impactful and better suited for this book than the definitions I found. Some of the synonyms for single include the following: individual; particular; special; original; separate; distinguished; one; exceptional; unique; unrivaled; only; and specific. Another word that I meditated on is whole. I found synonyms for it as well and they include: full; perfect; total; accomplished; completed; fixed; in one piece; rounded; fulfilled; integral; entire; and Alpha and Omega. I was fascinated by this list of empowering words and developed my own definitions of single which helped me to evolve in my conceptualization of the single experience:

Single: (n)
1. *unrivaled individual with a unique set of characteristics, talents, skills and abilities that sets them apart for a specific life purpose;*
2. *a whole, exceptional being, who is self-confident and content with her life;*
3. *an independent person who is more than capable of effectually taking care of oneself.*

Singleness: (v)
to engage in holistic well-being, fixed on living exceptionally as an integral member of society.

As you process how you love yourself for the next forty-five days, I encourage you to actively develop your own definitions for single and singleness so that you can reframe your single experience and embrace it with all your spirit, soul and body. Take your time in this section. Meditate on each question and allow yourself to feel and think deeply on matters concerning your soul. When you have a firm grasp on what it means and feels like to practice self-love, it will become an effortless practice and there will be an overflow of love in your life that will inevitably draw people with a similar flow.

One of the basic tenets of the Social Work profession is to start where the client is at. This basically means that as the Social Worker works on establishing a rapport with the client, they do so with respect for the dignity and worth of the individual, their life experiences, needs and expectations. It also means that the social worker doesn't allow their preconceived notions about where they think a client could or ought to be to interfere with the treatment process by setting intervention goals they simply aren't ready for. This is one of the ways a social worker practices compassion. In this, and subsequent vantage points, you will answer questions about compassion, grace, forgiveness and mercy. Compassion is simply action-oriented love. To be compassionate is to empathize with another person's experience and then actively seek to mitigate their suffering. When you turn compassion inward, you are activating the love within your spiritual being which then actively searches your soul and body to help you heal throughout. Compassion unleashes love, which in turn releases healing, because there is a recognition of the pain you're enduring and its impact on each part of your being. As you continuously and actively pursue deeper knowledge of self, you will be reminded of traumatic experiences you had dissociated from and make the connection between those experiences and your current patterns of thought, emotions, self-talk and behavior. Furthermore, this understanding allows you to understand why you believe and value the things you do, why you are who you are, and how you were able to enter one or more self-dishonoring relationships that led you to a dead-end.

The purpose of the questions you will answer in *How I Love Myself* section is to turn your compassion inward which self-love is. So, as you learn to meet yourself where you are at do so with respect and dignity for yourself. Be intentional about reading and responding to the questions, and practice accepting and embracing your unique thoughts, feelings and experiences that have formed you into the amazing person you are today. Set aside your judgments about where you think you should be in your life and allow yourself to be present so that the time that doesn't exist - your past and your future - doesn't overtake you and keep you feeling down. From healing, forgiveness is derived, and from that, mercy. Turn it all inward as you engage in trauma-informed reflection and know that this heartbreak, like all pain you've endured before it, shall pass.

DAY 1:

Who am I?

DAY 2:

How do I love myself?

DAY 3:

What do I love about being me?

DAY 4:

What do I think are the core components of this self-love and how do I implement them into my daily life?

DAY 5:

What would it take for me to cultivate deep, passionate and unshakeable feelings of self-love? Name ten ways to do this.

DAY 6:

I can identify ten intrinsic motivators and ten extrinsic motivators that would help me let go of my ex and the memories of my past relationship. breakup?

DAY 7:

I can identify ten personal strengths and ten related benefits of possessing these strengths. How can I develop them to make me even better?

DAY 8:

*Who are five people I can lean on to support me as my heart recovers?
What is one way each of these people can uniquely support me?*

DAY 9:

What are some ways that I may be withholding self-love because of this breakup?

DAY 10:

What are seven things I can do to start practicing self-love again?

DAY 11:

What relationship patterns have I noticed since I first started dating? How does this make me feel?

I AM Collage

Self-Love Focus: Positive Self-Talk

Time Required: 30+ Minutes

Purpose:

To use "I Am" statements to affirm oneself.

Materials Needed:

Magazines and newspapers, construction paper, scissors, glue stick, markers, glitter and all your other favorite art supplies.

Instructions:

    Decorate/draw the words "I Am" and put them at the center of your canvas. Peruse the magazines and newspapers for clippings that describe your positive traits, e.g., I am intelligent, sexy, philanthropic, artistic, an author, fantastic mother, etc. Cut out as many adjectives as you desire and glue them around "I Am".

    There are several other ways to design your "I Am" collage, build yours according to your heart's desire. When finished, hang the design on your wall as a daily reminder of your magnificence. Speak your "I Am's" out loud and with conviction, to keep you feeling inspired and manifest your best self.

DAY 12:

What are the desires of my heart that only God and myself are aware of?

DAY 13:

These are five practical things I can do so that the tangible desires of my heart can be fulfilled. How can I practice faith while I wait for my intangible desires to be fulfilled?

DAY 14:

If I gave myself all the types of attention and care that I've given my past lovers, what would that look like and how would I feel about myself?

DAY 15:

How can I use this time alone to prioritize my needs for self-improvement?

DAY 16:

How does my mental and emotional health equip me to be successfully single and overcome the pain and disappointments of this experience?

DAY 17

How does my spirituality equip me to be successfully single and overcome the pain and disappointments of this experience?

DAY 18:

How do I treat myself with compassion and grace?

DAY 19:

What habits, beliefs, thoughts, feelings and history am I holding on to?

DAY 20:

How do I show myself forgiveness and mercy?

DAY 21:

How do I treat myself (spirit, soul and body) with respect and honor?

Develop Your Personal Vision and Mission Statements

Self-Love Focus: Intentional Living

Vision statements are inspirational and grandiose, they function as a guide, and are written with long-term plans in mind. No vision is too big.

Mission statements are purpose driven; they identify what you do, who you do it for, and how you do it. Mission statements articulate how the vision will come to pass, thus making the vision more attainable. See the examples below that I developed for myself to get you started and then write your own personal vision and mission statements on the next page. Carry your vision and mission statements with you to help you stay focused on your purpose.

Vision Statement Example:

I will walk in wisdom and purpose. I will live authentically in all my ways, and experience lifelong, holistic prosperity and vitality, so that I may be healthy and whole all the days of my life.

Mission Statement Example:

I consciously choose to live a quality life by:

Seeking constantly to develop my leadership potential via training and self-reflection so that my soul may align with God's wisdom, so that this wisdom guides my behaviors.

I will effectually utilize the gifts, talents, knowledge, skills and abilities that God bestowed upon me so that I can walk in and on purpose, to make a difference in this world as a child of God.

My Personal Vision	My Personal Mission

DAY 22:

What are twenty things I can do right now to help me release my toxic feelings?

DAY 23:

How do I love and nurture my body?

DAY 24:

How do I love and nurture my spirit?

DAY 25:

How do I love and nurture my soul?

DAY 26:

What are five things I can do to feel comfortable and secure being alone?

DAY 27:

What makes me happy? How do I know when I am experiencing happiness?

DAY 28:

What gives me joy? How do I know when I am experiencing joy?

DAY 29:

What am I passionate about?

DAY 30:

What are ten ways I can practice mindfulness daily?

DAY 31:

What are twenty things I am grateful for?

Mirror, Mirror...

Self-Love Focus: Body Love

Time Required: *15* + Minutes

Purpose:

To develop a strong sense of body love and appreciation

Materials Needed:

Full-length mirror, your favorite outfit and fragrance, and beauty supplies.

Instructions:

- Beautify yourself as if you're going to have one of the most romantic evenings of your life.

- After you're dressed, stand before a full-length mirror and take a hard look at yourself. Feel every part of your body, inhale your fragrance on your wrists, massage your hair, caress your lips and look yourself in the eyes.

- Describe the following and write your experience on the next page:

  o Everything you love about the way you look

  o Everything you love about the way you smell

  o Everything you love about the way your skin feels

  o Notice your breathing, how relaxed do you feel?

- Slowly remove each article of clothing and repeat the exercise nude.

  o What feelings, if any, are different from those you experienced when you were clothed? Explain.

  o What do you need to do to fall in love with your body as is?

DAY 32:

What are some ways I can express gratitude and thanks every day? Why is it important for me to do this?

DAY 33:

What are my core values? How does my life reflect these values?

DAY 34:

What are my spiritual and/or religious beliefs?
How does my life reflect these beliefs?

DAY 35:

What are at least five of my most attractive physical characteristics?

DAY 36:

What are at least five most attractive characteristics of my personality?

DAY 37:

How would I describe my communication style? How does this work for me?

DAY 38:

What are thirty life-affirming statements I can say to myself to feel encouraged?

DAY 39:

When do I feel most confident?
What can I do to ensure these positive feelings persist?

DAY 40:

When do I feel least confident? What can I do differently so that my least confident feelings can be transformed into confident feelings?

DAY 41:

Who and/or what inspires me? Why?

My Feelings Chart

Self-Love Focus: Self-Awareness

For each emotion identified in the chart, identify five symptoms that reveal when you are feeling a certain way. Then name three things you need from others when you feel the way you do.

Emotions	Five Symptoms	Three Needs
Aroused		
Surprised		
Exhausted		
Goofy		
Hurt		
Sick		

Disgusted		
Satisfied		
Angry		
Jealous		
Bored		
Curious		
Ashamed		
Afraid		

DAY 42:

What are my top five priorities in life right now? Why?

DAY 43:

What are the wildest dreams I have for my life? What are five practical steps that I can take to get started on achieving my wildest dreams today?

DAY 44:

What are five opportunities that await me since my relationship ended?

DAY 45:

How comfortable am I with the possibility of being in love with someone else?

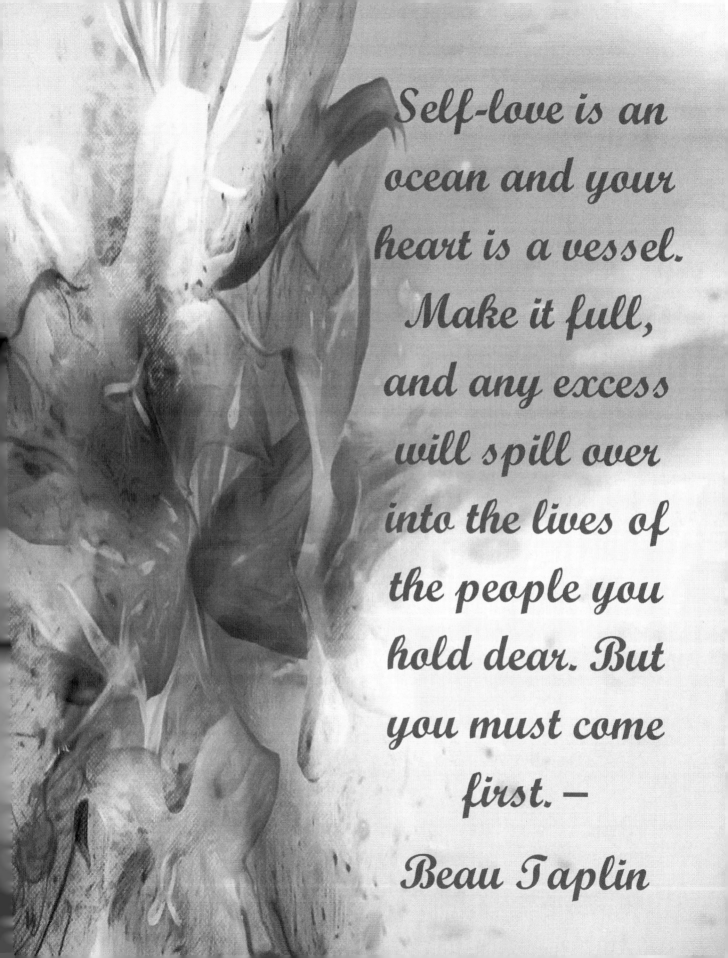

HOW I LOVED YOU

Seven years ago, an article was published on the Marie Claire website titled "7 Types of Breakups Ranked by Recovery Time[1]." The author, Rich Santos, identified seven reasons for breakups that many of us have experienced and ranked them from least painful - reason number seven, "The Mutual Breakup," to most painful - reason number one, "The Blind Side". The author hypothesizes that the type of breakup will determine the amount of time required for recovery. I have experienced five of the seven types of breakups and I would argue that the author's hypothesis is valid. There is sufficient evidence, from my experience alone, to support a conclusion that certain types of breakups hurt more than others and thus the individual's need for recovery time increases or decreases accordingly. Nevertheless, pain is pain and regardless why our relationships end, there is always a time when we look back and reflect on what was or might have been if circumstances were different or even if we had met our former partners at a different time. It's important to reflect on past relationships. Being removed from the situation gives you an opportunity to take an objective look at the role you and your partner fulfilled in developing your relationship, deconstructing the relationship and eventually ending it. The purpose of *How I Loved You* is to empathize with your ex. You will reflect on how you presented yourself to your former partner and what it was that you contributed to the relationship and took away from it that may have impacted them in a lasting positive or negative way.

Depending on what types of traumatic experiences you may have endured in the relationship, it can be rather difficult to look back without sinking into the pain you experienced in your relationship and allowing it to identify who you are and what you're worth. For the next forty-five days practice using your safety and self-care plans that you'll find in this section to be sure you aren't overwhelmed by possible triggers. The truth is, sometimes breakups are a tremendous relief because our relationships seem to thwart us into the depths of hell via physical, emotional, financial and other forms of abuse or neglect, and other times, despite what we've been through, the break up feels much worse. The trauma we endure when we are romantically involved with someone makes a very powerful and negative impression on our self-regard, that is why it is imperative to develop positive coping skills and learn how to feel safe and satisfied alone. There is a tendency, especially for women, to internalize our experiences and accept all the mess we go through as confirmation of our lack of value and worth, and so we buy into negative stories from people about who we are, when at minimum, we should only rent the story just to see what we may or may not have done that

---

[1] Santos, R. (2010, February 11). 7 Types of Breakups ranked by recovery time. *Marie Claire*. Retrieved from http://www.marieclaire.com/sex-love/a3865/types-of-breakups/

made them think the story was worth selling. *How I Loved You* is not about internalizing anything. It's about learning more about yourself and developing your ability to practice self-compassion, forgiveness, grace and mercy. Only when we learn to recapture our identities by learning about and loving who we are, by speaking life affirmations to ourselves daily, and by disowning the harmful stories our partners tell us about ourselves, can we be free in our thoughts and emotions and finally begin to heal.

I believe there are many types of nurturers and would never limit a woman's nurturing instinct to mothering. That said, I do think that our instincts to nurture can sometimes keep us in toxic or less than perfect relationships way past their expiration date because we are so focused on nurturing others and in turn, neglect to nurture ourselves. We want our relationships to flourish, so we make every effort we can to make it work and when it doesn't, we are left feeling depleted and irrelevant. I want you to be able to recognize your relevance, with and without a partner, and learn how to fill yourself with the love you that you long to share with the world. When you finally understand who you become and how you behave when you're in a relationship, and whether this aligns with the core components of self-love you identified in the *How I Love Myself* section, then you can make healthy improvements that honor your spirit, soul and body and that of all others. I want you to feel strong and secure enough to be able to prioritize your self-care and then make time to nurture other people, so dig into this experience with all your human being and own it. Whether you broke up with your partner and are experiencing feelings of regret and guilt, or they broke up with you and you are feeling rejected and ashamed, you must deal honestly with your thoughts and feelings so that you can let go of what's happened, heal from the inside-out and successfully move on.

To reference my mentor and dear friend, Teresa, you need to climb on the balcony and allow yourself to witness every moment of your relationship with an eagle eye objective point of view. As you answer the questions in the *How I Loved You* section, think about how your partner may have experienced you; how you experienced yourself in hindsight; and allow yourself to finally hear and understand all the feedback you received from others about how you were in your relationship, and then write the truth so that you can set free to do differently and become a better person. Brene Brown said, "When we find the courage to share our experiences and the compassion to hear others tell their stories, we force shame out of hiding and end the silence." There is no shame in acknowledging your imperfections and the need for personal growth, and even if your ex never gets to experience the better version of you, at least you get to walk with integrity and exude confidence unlike they've ever seen. You got this!

DAY 46:

How did we meet? What was my first impression of my ex?

DAY 47:

What factors contributed to my choice to get involved with my former partner?

DAY 48:

How did I go against my intuition by getting in this relationship? Were there any red flags in the beginning that I chose to ignore? What were the consequences of that decision?

DAY 49:

How did I reveal my true self to my partner? What aspects did I withhold?

DAY 50:

What are three things we did to establish trust and honesty in our relationship? How did it turn out?

Baggage Claim

Self-Love Focus: Accountability and Responsibility

On each suitcase name one thing that you are bringing into a relationship. Identify your assets and liabilities. After you've labeled each bag, review them to see whether you carry more baggage with liabilities or more baggage with assets. Write about this on the next page.

Baggage Claim

DAY 51:

What were my intentions and expectations for my last relationship? What impact did this have on the relationship?

DAY 52:

What are five ways I knew I was ready to be in a relationship?

DAY 53:

How well did I know my former partner? What did I know?

DAY 54:

What kind of feedback did I receive from my former partner about their experience dating me?

DAY 55:

Based on the feedback I received from my partner about dating me,
how do I think I am fit and unfit to be in a positive intimate relationship?

DAY 56:

How did the unresolved issues of my past interfere with my ability to have a healthy relationship with my former partner?

DAY 57:

How is my choice to be sexually active with my partners affecting my judgment? What would happen if I waited to have sex with my partner?

DAY 58:

What is it about practicing celibacy that makes me uncomfortable? Why?

DAY 59:

How do my dating behaviors align with my core values and beliefs? How don't they?

DAY 60:

Is it possible that I settled for my former relationship? In what ways?

A Letter to My Ex:

♥ *Self-Love Focus: Catharsis*

♥ *Let this letter serve as a catharsis for you.*

♥ *Write the letter from your heart.*

♥ *Use it to get closure and say everything that's been on your mind.*

♥ *Do not send this letter to your ex.*

♥ *Use "I" language to express how you felt when certain things happened in your relationship and how you feel now.*

　　o *Example: I felt hurt when I had to eat dinner alone after preparing a nice meal. It made me feel unwanted and unappreciated. I want to be with someone who values my time and the effort I put in to spend it with them. I feel like now I am ready to share these thoughts with someone new.*

♥ *Now that our relationship is over, I feel…*

♥ *I am better now because…*

DAY 61:

How did our relationship end? What does that the ending reveal about the kind of relationship we had?

DAY 62:

When did I first recognize that there was a problem in our relationship? How did I respond to this problem?

DAY 63:

What was my role in the relationship leading up to the breakup?

DAY 64:

What did I do and/or say in the relationship that I wish I hadn't?
What difference might it have made?

DAY 65:

What didn't I do and/or say in the relationship that I wish I had? What difference might it have made?

DAY 66:

What are ten beliefs I have about men?

How might these beliefs shape my intimate relationship dynamics?

DAY 67:

What are ten beliefs I have about women?
How might these beliefs shape my intimate relationship dynamics?

DAY 68:

How did I show my former partner compassion and grace?

DAY 69:

How did I show my former partner forgiveness and mercy?

DAY 70:

What needs, and desires did my former partner express to me that I didn't fulfill? In what ways was I ill-equipped to meet those needs and desires?

My Breakup Safety Plan

Self-Love Focus: Self-Regulation

Things That May Trigger Me	These Are My Warning Signs
When I Am Feeling…	*I Will Self-Soothe By…*

When Self-Soothing is Challenging or I Have a Crisis, I Can Ask These People for Help:

Name	Contact Information

DAY 71:

What did I learn about myself in this relationship and can now do better because of this experience?

DAY 72:

Do I still desire my former partner or other exes? Who?
What sort of thoughts, feelings and physical experiences do I remember about
my ex that keeps me longing for them?

DAY 73:

How did I respond when my former partner was emotionally vulnerable with me?

DAY 74:

What are the different ways I hurt my former partner?
(Physically, emotionally, mentally, financially, etc.)

DAY 75:

How did I take I responsibility for the way I affected my former partner? Did I apologize and repent? What were the results?

DAY 76:

What are some regrets I have about how things happened in my former relationship and how it ended?

DAY 77:

What is best for my former partner?   How do I know this?

DAY 78:

How did I l show appreciation and respect for the health, wellness and strengthening of my former partner's body?

DAY 79:

How did I show appreciation and respect for the health, wellness and strengthening of my former partner's spirit?

DAY 80:

How did I show appreciation and respect for the health, wellness and strengthening of my former partner's soul?

My Self-Care Action Plan

Self-Love Focus: Self-Care

Physical Self-Care *Write down your action plan to take care of your body. Include everything you think you need to ensure your physical health. Examples include create a weekly meal plan, exercise 45 minutes per day, four days a week, drink 82oz water per day.*	
Spiritual Self-Care *Write down your action plan to take care of your spiritual health. Include everything you think you need to ensure your spiritual health. Examples include pray 10 minutes a day, meditate 20 minutes every two days, attend church weekly.*	
Emotional Self-Care *Write down your action plan to take care of your emotional health. Include everything you think you need to develop and strengthen your emotional health. Examples include journal daily, speak life-affirming statements in mirror each day, practice gratitude.*	
Psychological Self-Care *Write down your action plan to take care of your mental health. Include everything that will help you establish peace and stability in your soul. Examples include participate in therapy monthly, volunteer for a charity, try something new.*	

Professional Self-Care

Write down your action plan to take care of your professional health. Include everything that will help you effectively manage self on the job, improve your relationships with colleagues, and help you reach your employment and career goals.

Financial Self-Care

Write down your action plan to take care of your finances. Include everything that will help you establish or strengthen your financial health. Examples include write short, medium and long-term SMART Financial Goals, create a budget, save 15% of every other paycheck.

Relationship Self-Care

Write down your action plan to take care of your relationships. Jot down the names of people you love and respect and then identify the ways you will maintain your relationships with them. Try to identify why these relationships are important to you.

Other Self-Care

Write down your action plan to take care of yourself in other ways not identified here. Examine your life to determine where the self-care gaps are and what you can do to achieve wholeness in these areas.

DAY 81:

If I learned that my former partner was involved with someone else, I would...

DAY 82:

Why might my former partner have been allowed to enter my life? What might have been the purpose for my entering theirs?

DAY 83:

How did I communicate my role in the demise of our relationship with my former partner?

DAY 84:

What did my former partner's family and friends think about me?

DAY 85:

How did I interact with my former partner's family and friends? How did these interactions effect our relationship?

DAY 86:

Did I ever desire to have a long-term, committed relationship with my former partner? If not, why did I stay in it?

DAY 87:

What did my former partner say that I needed to change so that we could have a better relationship? How can I use this feedback in the future?

DAY 88:

When did I know our relationship was over?

DAY 89:

Is it possible for me and my former partner to get back together and make our relationship work for the long-haul? What would have to be done differently for the relationship to work?

DAY 90:

What are ten lessons I've learned since we broke up?

How I Feel Safe in Romantic Partnerships

Self-Love Focus: Healthy Boundaries

Use the **SAFETY** acronym below to identify what needs must be fulfilled for you to feel safe with your partner in a relationship. **Socially:** what do you need to feel safe with your partner in public or when interacting with others? **Affectionately:** what do you need to feel physically safe with your partner when they touch you intimately in public settings versus in private settings? **Financially:** what financial standards must be fulfilled so that you may feel stable and secure in a romantic partnership? **Emotionally:** what are some ways you know that you feel emotionally safe in a romantic relationship? **Thoughts:** what are some ways that you feel safe to express your thoughts in a romantic partnership? **You:** what are some general things you need to feel safe in a romantic partnership?

Socially	
Affectionately	
Financially	
Emotionally	
Thoughts	
You	

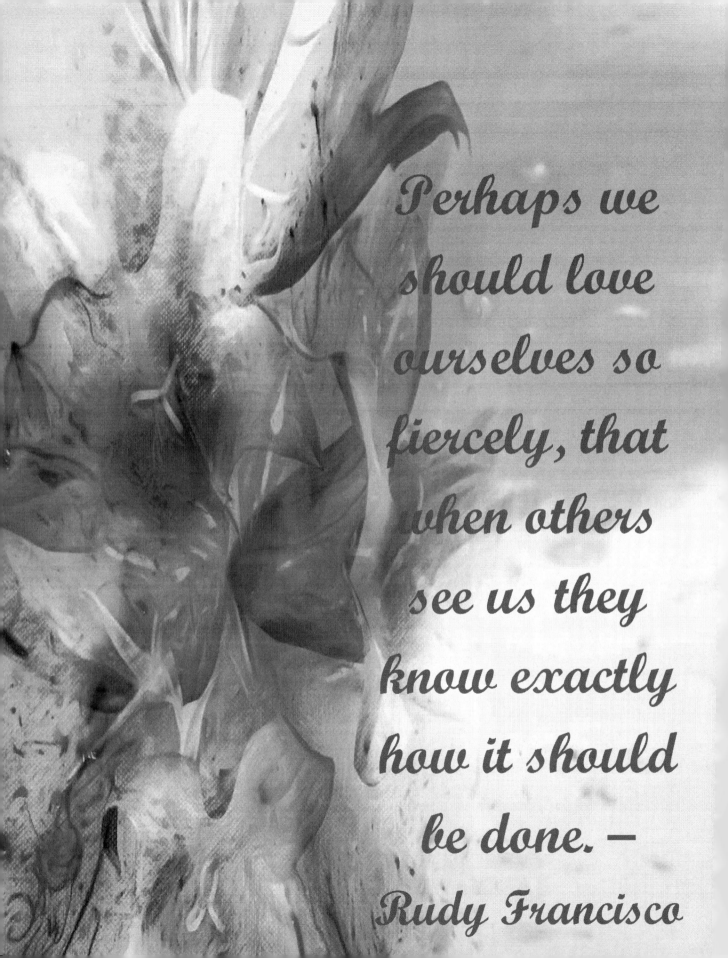

Perhaps we should love ourselves so fiercely, that when others see us they know exactly how it should be done. — Rudy Francisco

HOW YOU LOVED ME

In the preface I told you that when you reached this vantage point, you would engage in solution-based venting. What does that mean, you ask? It means that you have been given an opportunity to vent about the problems you experienced in your relationship, and then you must get back on your balcony to objectively discern the problem so that you can develop solutions to improve your life.

Because you're using the *Complete 180* personal workbook and journal to process your thoughts and feelings after your breakup, I think it's safe to assume that your emotions are poignant and that you're willing to do almost anything to get your mind and heart back on track, which means you want to solve problems. Therefore, *How You Loved Me* contains questions similar to *How I Loved You* so that you can recognize the mirroring behaviors, thoughts and feelings you and your ex presented to each other in your relationship. You will begin to understand the meaning you gave to the way your partner treated you and how that, in turn, effected the way you see yourself. On the flip-side, you will take an empathetic stance so that you can understand how your interpretation of your experiences with your partner effected the way you perceived them and treated them in response.

Trauma is something we tend to think about after we find ourselves suffering from the external consequences of it. Amid traumatic experiences, we may not even recognize the frequency and depth at which we are being abused or abusing others because trauma is like an impenetrable cloud of darkness that surrounds us so that we can't see but are readily capable of reacting to triggers that cause us to lose ourselves and hurt many people along the way since we are blind to them and their experience of us. In other words, your ex may not be able or willing to take personal accountability and responsibility for the hurt or harm they caused you, and as disappointing and upsetting as that may be, you cannot allow yourself to become obsessed with the idea of being recompensed for how you were abused. What you can do, and will do in this section, is allow yourself to step into your ex's shoes and walk their journey with you. As you reflect on your partner's maltreatment of you, understand that you are not giving them permission to dishonor your spirit, soul or body. You are not apologizing for them or giving them excuses. Instead you are just owning your experience with them so that you can reclaim your power and finally learn to recognize the lessons your relationship afforded you and to appreciate your breakup because it signifies new and better beginnings.

I chose to emphasize trauma in this section because I recognize from my own life experiences how deeply impactful traumatic experiences can be and the way it navigates our lives, often without our knowledge and permission. After my ex-fiancée and I broke up for the last time and both decided to be single, I had plenty of time to think about all the baggage from my childhood and traumatic adult experiences I carried into my relationship and poured onto her. I had spent years convinced that I was healed from my past and could effectively manage my present triggers. Then after our breakup, I finally acknowledged that the years of traumatic experiences I endured had molded me into a woman bound by fear of rejection, who was cynical and distrusting, and felt worthless and irrelevant, and that I couldn't receive or give love no matter how desperately I wanted it. I knew something had to change and that it had to be me, so, I asked God to search my heart and reveal all that was afflicting my soul, so I could forgive myself for what I've done and who I've been to myself and others, and then demonstrate forgiveness to other people who hurt me in any way.

Regardless of your life experiences thus far, trauma can happen to anyone, at any time, and is unique to everyone. Therefore, even if you didn't experience a pattern of abuse or neglect in your relationship, you may have experienced moments of abuse or dishonor to your spirit, soul, or body, and may, otherwise, still be carrying the weight of past experiences into your relationships. The sooner you recognize how trauma has affected you, the more equipped you will be to address trauma-related issues that impact you internally and externally, and then begin to heal. If you didn't experience abuse in your relationship, but you are feeling overwhelmed by disappointment and sadness because of missed opportunities in your relationship, then own those feelings as well and express gratitude for what you learned and can take away from your experience with this person. Be intentional about reading and responding to the journal prompts. When you do this, you will gain a greater awareness of self in relation to your ex, get clarity about how the relationship impacted you and prepare yourself to release forgiveness, grace, mercy and compassion to your ex, so that you can finally let go and move forward and make changes for your personal betterment.

"Forgiveness doesn't excuse their behavior. Forgiveness prevents their behavior from destroying your heart," -
Anonymous

DAY 91:

Who was my former partner in real life compared with who I thought or believed they could be?

DAY 92:

Was I committed to who my former partner actually was or my fantasy about who they could be?

DAY 93:

What efforts did my ex make to connect with me emotionally and mentally? What are ten ways I know that I am connecting with someone emotionally and mentally?

DAY 94:

The strengths and weaknesses of my former partner include the following:

DAY 95:

What did I like about my former partner?
What does this reveal about my core values and beliefs?

DAY 96:

What didn't I like about my former partner?
What does this reveal about my core values and beliefs?

DAY 97:

*What did my family and friends think about my former partner?
How do I know?*

DAY 98:

How did my former partner interact with my family and friends? How did these interactions effect our relationship?

DAY 99:

How did my former partner talk to me and about me?
How did this make me feel?

DAY 100:

What are the different ways my former partner hurt me? (Physically, emotionally, mentally, financially, etc.)

Spring Clean Your Life

Self-Care Focus: New Beginnings

Home	**Heart**
♥ Rearrange your furniture.	♥ Find a therapist who specializes in intimate partnerships to help you effectively process your emotions.
♥ Redesign your space with different accent pieces, paint the walls, change the pillows on the couch.	
♥ Discard all photos of your ex — even the ones that have you in them looking good.	♥ Utilize the no-contact rule in thirty-day increments until you completely lose your desire to contact your ex or check them out on social media.
♥ Clean your mattress and other furniture fabrics to remove the fragrance of your ex.	♥ Fellowship with family and friends to strengthen those relationships and help you get your mind off your ex.
♥ Get rid of your ex's belongings. (If there is a safe mutual friend you can reach out to who can collect your ex's belongings, call them, otherwise, throw them away).	♥ Cry when you need to and then get up and keep living.
	♥ Confide in someone who can be trusted and loves you and can help you heal.

Health	**Hope**
♥ Begin that new fitness regimen you've been talking about.	♥ Participate in spiritual and/or religious activities to inspire hope for your future and help you live intentionally every day.
♥ Avoid drinking alcohol or consuming other drugs while you're still healing.	♥ Set SMART goals for different areas of your life: financial, physical, relationship, health and wellness, etc.
♥ Take a walk outside or practice deep breathing exercises for fifteen minutes every time you feel like contacting your ex.	♥ Get a beauty makeover and/or change your hair to create a new look.
♥ Set a sleep schedule and use an app on your phone to remind you when to go to bed and set an alarm to wake you up.	♥ Take the time to learn who you are apart from your relationship and make practicing self-love your top priority.

DAY 101:

How did I my ex take responsibility for the way they treated me?
Did they apologize and repent? What were the results?

DAY 102:

How have my relationship standards evolved overtime? Name ten standards you now have that you never did before.

DAY 103:

How did my former partner inspire me or bring out the best in me? What were the consequences of these inspiring experiences?

DAY 104:

*How did my former partner dishearten me or bring out the worst in me?
What were the consequences of these disheartening experiences?*

DAY 105:

If I could transfer the best qualities of my former partner into my ideal mate, I would describe my new partner like...

DAY 106:

How do I know that my former partner loved me?
Did I willingly stay in a relationship with someone I knew didn't love me?
Explain.

DAY 107:

How did my ex love and nurture my body?

DAY 108:

How did my ex love and nurture my spirit?

DAY 109:

How did my ex love and nurture my soul?

DAY 110:

What would it take for my ex to change for the better?
Why does this matter to me?

A Love Letter to Self:

♥ *Self-Love Focus:* Positive Self-Regard

♥ *Write a passionate and honest letter from the heart about how in love with yourself you are.*

♥ *Closure:* say everything that's been on your mind to provide yourself closure from your previous relationship.

♥ *Affirmation:* include all the things you need to hear to feel good about yourself but sought from others.

♥ *Accomplishments:* identify all the great things about who you are that have allowed you to experience so many blessings in life and then write how you will achieve abundant blessings.

♥ *Plan:* write a plan for your future expressing how you will continue to practice self-love and self-compassion.

♥ *Reminder:* in case you tend to forget, write a few reminders about why you are so loveable.

♥ *Read:* mail a copy of the letter to yourself and read it aloud when you are feeling down.

DAY 111:

What kind of issues from my former partner's past interfered with their ability to have a healthy relationship with me? How so?

DAY 112:

As I reflect deeply on our time together, do I really want to get back together with my ex? Why or why not?

DAY 113:

What attracted me to my ex?
(Physically, emotionally, spiritually, psychologically)

DAY 114:

What do I really miss about my former partner? (Describe emotional, psychological, financial, sexual or other needs). Based on this, is it fair for me to pursue the relationship again?

DAY 115:

These are ten reasons I would never get involved with my ex again…

DAY 116:

How does my ex trigger me? What can I do to prevent myself from reacting in ways that may cause myself and/or my ex harm of any kind?

DAY 117:

When I spent time with my former partner, did I feel more energized or depressed afterward? Explain.

DAY 118:

Does my former partner seem to be happier and better off without me? How does that make me feel?

DAY 119:

If I could say anything to my ex right now to receive closure, I would say...

DAY 120:

What physical, emotional and psychological needs were fulfilled by having sex with my former partner? Is there another way to get these needs met without sex right now? Explain.

Home Spa Day

♥ Self-Love Focus: Intrapersonal Intimacy

♥ Light some candles and set them up around your bathtub and on the nightstands in your bedroom.

♥ Use your favorite nail polish to give yourself a mani-pedi.

♥ Make your own detox water or drink some detox tea.

♥ Deep cleanse your face and apply a facial mask.

♥ Take a nice warm bath that has your favorite bath beads or essential oils in it.

♥ Put your comfiest robe in the dryer for a few minutes and put it on after your bath.

♥ Check out Pinterest for more cozy home spa day ideas.

DAY 121:

These are five reasons I felt relieved after our relationship ended:

DAY 122:

Was my ex trustworthy? Explain.
How does this effect my thoughts and feelings concerning them?

DAY 123:

How did my ex make me feel heard and understood?
Regardless, what are ten ways I know that I am being heard and understood?

DAY 124:

What did I gain from being in my former relationship?

DAY 125:

How did my former partner make me feel valued and appreciated?

If they didn't, what are then ways you need to feel valued and appreciated by your partner?

DAY 126:

How did your former partner make you feel sexy and attractive?
If they didn't, what are seven ways you'd know your partner thought you were sexy and attractive?

DAY 127:

How did your former partner stimulate you intellectually? Describe your intellectual needs and interests.

DAY 128:

How did I appreciate my former partner?
Were they aware of this appreciation?

DAY 129:

What did outsiders observe and communicate about the way my ex treated me? How did I respond to their observations and feedback?

DAY 130:

How did my former partner respond or react when our relationship ended? How did this make me feel?

Compliment Jar

Self-Love Focus: *Self-Confidence*

Purpose:

To develop your ability to recognize and appreciate your strengths and positive characteristics.

Materials Needed:

Large glass jar with lid

Colorful slips of paper

Instructions:

Write down every compliment you receive from anyone. When you get home, transfer the compliment to the colorful slips of paper and put it in the jar. When you are having an emotionally challenging day, reach into the jar, pull out a compliment and read it aloud in the mirror.

DAY 131:

If I reached out to my ex and learned that they were no longer interested in seeing me or communicating with me again, what sorts of thoughts and feelings might I experience? How could I then move on?

DAY 132:

Do I think my ex might have learned anything as a result of dating me that may benefit them in the future? Explain.

DAY 133:

What did I learn about my former partner as a result of our relationship?

HOW I NEED TO BE LOVED

Heartbreak has a way of opening our eyes to the reality of who we've been, what we've done and what we believe. If we take ownership of the experience and allow ourselves to understand the purpose of our pain, then we become better equipped to wield it for our personal development. Complete 180 was written so that you could wield your pain for the improvement of your life. From the final vantage point of *How I Need to be Loved*, you will take inventory of your soul to discern what it is that you truly need in a relationship and learn what healing and liberation is required for you to qualify for this need to be met. No matter what kind of pain you experienced in your previous relationship; despite how much it hurts right now and makes you believe you can't breathe and function without your ex; even on those days when it feels like your former partner owes you something for whatever way(s) they dishonored your spirit, soul and body, the truth remains, that you are the common denominator in each painful experience you went through and it's time to do something different.

As you've been instructed in every other vantage point thus far, take the time to meditate over each journal prompt presented to you each day. Allow yourself to be shut away from anything that will detract you from your purpose, which is healing, so that you can assess the state of your heart and learn how different your actual needs are from your current desires. If you completed the vantage points prior to this with mindfulness and integrity, then you have been equipped with the internal resources you need to help you conquer these last forty-five days of your complete 180 transformation. If you own this time as a single person you will live in wholeness for the rest of your life, with or without a partner. Be blessed.

DAY 134:

What are my core relationship values?

DAY 135:

What are ten ways I know that my partnership aligns with my relationship values?

DAY 136:

What is my vision for a lifelong partnership?

DAY 137:

What are ten ways I know that my relationship aligns with my vision for lifelong partnership?

DAY 138:

What is my love language?

DAY 139:

What are five ways I can effectively communicate my needs and desires to my partner?

DAY 140:

How do I know when I am infatuated with someone?
(Describe physical, emotional and mental symptoms).

Reframing

Self-Love Focus: Positive Reframing

Instead of this...	Try this...
♥ I can't live without my ex	♥ I will create a new life for myself.
♥ Nobody will ever love me	♥ I am lovable with or without a partner.
♥ Men just can't be trusted	♥ I will learn to trust by trusting
♥ I will never get over this pain.	♥ I need time to heal and that's okay.
♥ Breaking up was a huge mistake.	♥ Breaking up was the healthiest decision we could make because…
♥ This was all my fault.	♥ We are both responsible for the development, destruction and demise of our relationship.
♥ I will never contact him again.	
♥ I could never do better than her.	♥ I will commit to taking it one day at a time until I finally see no need to contact my ex.
♥ He'll never find someone as wonderful as I am.	♥ If I was able to attract someone with the good qualities my ex has, then I know I can attract another person with those good qualities and more.
♥ I'm just too much for her to handle.	
	♥ If my ex was able to attract someone as wonderful as me, then I know he can attract someone else just as wonderful or better, and that's okay.
	♥ I am enough and will meet the right person who compliments me.

DAY 141:

How do I know I am experiencing mature love for someone?
(Describe physical, emotional and mental symptoms).

DAY 142:

Do I believe it is possible to fall out of love with someone? If so, how do I know this has happened? (Describe physical, emotional and mental symptoms).

DAY 143:

Looking back at my last five relationships, I can see the following pattern(s):

DAY 144:

How much time do I expect to spend with my partner?
How would this impact career, social and family obligations?

DAY 145:

These are ten ways I know that I am in a fulfilling relationship:

DAY 146:

What marital or long-term relationships do I admire? Who are these people? What is it about them and their relationship(s) that I respect?

DAY 147:

How do my dating patterns emulate the types of relationships I admire?

DAY 148:

In what ways do my moral and ethical beliefs shape my sexual behaviors and preferences?

DAY 149:

On a scale of one to ten, with ten being very comfortable and one being very uncomfortable, how comfortable do I feel about abstaining from sex until marriage? What are the fears I have about doing this?

DAY 150:

In what ways do my moral and ethical beliefs shape my views about monogamy and/or marriage? Do I want to be in a monogamous relationship and/or married? Why?

21 Days of Self-Care

Self-Love Focus: Self-Care Habituation

Day 1: Call your best friend.

Day 2: Host a game night with your family.

Day 3: Color in your favorite coloring book.

Day 4: Sing & dance wildly to your favorite songs.

Day 5: Take a walk on a nature trail.

Day 6: Make a vision board.

Day 7: Read your favorite book at a park.

Day 8: Take a free fitness class.

Day 9: Do some deep breathing exercises.

Day 10: Try mindful eating during your lunch.

Day 11: Attend a religious service.

Day 12: Watch your favorite comedy.

Day 13: Try a new healthy recipe.

Day 14: Have a technology-free day.

Day 15: Pick some flowers from a garden.

Day 16: Take a bubble bath.

Day 17: Sleep in.

Day 18: Meditate and/or pray for 20 minutes.

Day 19: Write down 31 things you are grateful for.

Day 20: Speak positive affirmations in the mirror.

Day 21: Get dressed up and take yourself on a date.

DAY 151:

These are ten benefits I get me from being in a relationship:

DAY 152:

These are ten benefits I get from being single:

DAY 153:

As I compare my ten benefits of being in a relationship versus being single, I am most attracted to the idea of being.... Explain.

DAY 154:

What are my beliefs and values concerning family? (my own parents, my partner's parents, my children, my partner's children, fostering, adoption, sibling relationships, extended family, etc.).

DAY 155:

What does commitment mean to me? What would this look like in my ideal relationship?

DAY 156:

I am unwilling to experience the following situations ever again in any relationship...

DAY 157:

What does it mean to "take it slow" or "go with the flow?" in a relationship? Do I know how to do this? Am I willing to do this?

DAY 158:

What are some of my relationship triggers?
How do I know that I have been triggered?

DAY 159:

What are ten things I need to feel psychologically safe with my partner?

DAY 160:

What are ten things I need to feel emotionally safe with my partner?

Love is not something we give or get; it is something that we nurture and grow. A connection that can only be cultivated between two people when it exists within each of them — we can only love others as much as we love ourselves. — Brene Brown

DAY 161:

What are ten things I need to feel physically safe with my partner?

DAY 162:

What are ten things I need to feel socially safe with my partner?

DAY 163:

How do I apologize and ask for forgiveness?
One example of my ability to do this is...

DAY 164:

How do I receive apologies and practice forgiveness?
One example of my ability to do this is...

DAY 165:

Am I comfortable communicating my sexual desires, fantasies, anxieties and insecurities with my partner? Why or why not?

DAY 166:

How would I like to be romanced in a relationship?
How do I romance my partners in relationships?

DAY 167:

How do I show vulnerability? If I am uncomfortable with vulnerability, what factors of my past might have influenced this fear?

DAY 168:

Am I willing to work on practicing vulnerability in my relationships? What would this entail?

DAY 169:

What kinds of childhood traumas did I experience and how does that effect my romantic relationships?

DAY 170:

What kinds of toxic stresses in adulthood do I experience and how do they affect my romantic relationships?

DAY 171:

What do I believe I deserve in a relationship? Why?

DAY 172:

Am I prepared to do the work to sustain a lifelong, healthy relationship? What are some practical things I can do to sustain a healthy relationship?

DAY 173:

How much money does my partner need to make for me to feel stable and secure? What kind of moral restrictions do I have concerning the way my partner earns their money?

DAY 174:

What qualities and characteristics do I consider to be irresistible in a prospective romantic partner?

DAY 175:

What qualities and characteristics do I consider to be absolute deal breakers?

DAY 176:

On a scale from one to ten, with ten being very important and one being not at all important, how important is it to me for my partner to share my spiritual values, beliefs and practices? Explain.

DAY 177:

On a scale from one to ten, with ten being very important and one being not at all important, how important is it to me for my partner to share my financial values, beliefs and practices? Explain.

DAY 178:

How can I uphold my sexual integrity while I am single? How will this impact my future lifelong partnership?

DAY 179:

What do I need to continue my journey of self-love and personal development?

DAY 180:

How will I know that I am healed?

NOW WHAT?

Congratulations! You made it to day 180 of the *Complete 180: A Journal for Cultivating Self-Love After a Breakup*. I hope the last 180 days have been a meaningful experience that have opened your eyes to your greatness and allowed you to fully embrace who you are as a single person.

I know that every day wasn't easy. You might have had a couple drinks and drunk-dialed your ex; you might have skipped a few questions in the journal because you didn't think they were relevant to your experience; you may have even avoided self-care because it somehow felt better to wallow in your pain…and that's okay. I did it too. This book was made for people who are in the process of healing. Processes take time and even if it's true that it takes twenty-one days to develop a habit and ninety days to create a lifestyle, you can't rely on time to heal your wounds, you must take ownership of the time and actively pursue holistic healing and wholeness. So, I challenge you for the next forty-five days to keep pursuing your healing. Although there are no more pages to complete in this book, I encourage you to keep referring to the prompts in each section as you gain more insight or even if you find yourself struggling with some of the ideas presented therein, and then write about them in another journal. Heck, purchase this one again and start the process over if you need to! Pull out your safety and self-care plans and carry them with you to help you effectively manage your emotions daily and make updates to these plans when you notice any psychological, emotional or spiritual changes that require you to take a different approach to your self-care and safety. Refer to a therapist or your list of social supports and contact them when you find yourself in an emotional or psychological crisis. Whatever you do, make self-love your priority.

To get you started I have provided you with forty-five ways to practice self-care for the next forty-five days - after you finish, add more and keep it going forever:

1. Get a massage.

2. Read for at least thirty minutes.

3. Download a deep breathing app and set it to use nightly.

4. Eat a few pieces of candy.

5. Pray for fifteen minutes.

6. Stretch for ten minutes.

7. Have coffee with someone who makes you laugh.

8. Plan for the week ahead.

9. Rent a bicycle and ride around your town.

10. Deep condition your hair.

11. List 50 things you're grateful for.

12. Apologize to someone you hurt.

13. List everything that made you smile in the last three days.

14. Watch your favorite reality show.

15. Bake a dessert to give to a coworker.

16. Take a nap.

17. Go for a walk outdoors on your lunch break.

18. Play board games with your family.

19. Work out to a fitness DVD or TV subscription/trial.

20. Update your safety plan.

21. Find ways to improve your hobby on Pinterest.

22. Rehearse your "I Am" statements in the mirror.

23. Research and then write down 21 inspirational quotes or passages.

24. Read an uplifting spiritual or religious book.

25. Download a meditation app and set it to use every morning.

26. Try bullet journaling.

27. Mindfully eat your favorite fruit and write about how you experienced it with all your senses.

28. Visit the city garden.

29. Call a friend you haven't talked to in a long time.

30. Write a new love letter to yourself.

31. Ask for something you want.

32. Bake some cookies to give your home a sweet smell.

33. Sit in your favorite room in the house and quietly admire the space.

34. Pray for fifteen minutes.

35. Finish a long overdue project.

36. Give someone a hug.

37. Go to the park and swing.

38. Find a free event in your city and attend it with a couple friends.

39. Try something new.

40. Listen to your favorite music and sing every song out loud.

41. Do some artwork: draw, paint, color.

42. Soak in a lavender and chamomile bath with soft music playing in the background.

43. Buy some new underwear.

44. Visit a library and check out a book you've wanted to read since childhood.

45. Create a new list of self-care ideas to use for the next 45 days.

And just because it's natural to wonder…When the time is right, and your spirit, soul and body are properly aligned for you to receive it, you will attract natural love into your life and you'll finally be able to witness, via the love of another being, all the unconditional love and favor you've shown yourself and have been graced with by God. For now, embrace your singleness by practicing gratitude and contentment for the time you have alone, and trust that "I Am" will not be denied.